Amazon founder Jeff Bezos

AMAZON

CREATIVE COMPANIES

SARA GILBERT

JAICO PUBLISHING HOUSE
Ahmedabad Bangalore Chennai
Delhi Hyderabad Kolkata Mumbai

Published by Jaico Publishing House
A-2 Jash Chambers, 7-A Sir Phirozshah Mehta Road
Fort, Mumbai - 400 001
jaicopub@jaicobooks.com
www.jaicobooks.com

Published in arrangement with
The Creative Company
2140 Howard Drive West,
North Mankato, MN 56003, USA

To be sold only in India, Bangladesh, Bhutan,
Pakistan, Nepal, Sri Lanka and the Maldives.

Design by Graham Morgan
Art direction by Tom Morgan
Edited by Jill Kalz

Images by Alamy (Kristoffer Tripplaar, Jack Young, WorldFoto), Getty (Joe Raedle, Johnny Milano/Bloomberg, Joshua Lott/Bloomberg, Justin Sullivan, Ken James/Bloomberg, Kevin Schafer, Michael Kovac, Paul Hawthorne, Ryder/Bloomberg. Spencer Platt, Thinkstock), Pexels (Anna Shvets, Erik Mclean, Stephanie Ho, ThisIsEngineering), Unsplash (Alexandra Tran, Andrew Stickelman, ANIRUDH, Anshu A, Christian Wiediger, engin akyurt, Kaitlyn Baker, rupixen.com, Vivint Solar), Wikimedia Commons (Acroterion, Bonnachoven, Mathieu Thouvenin, Michael Fleischhacker)

AMAZON
ISBN 978-93-49358-05-8

First Jaico Impression: 2025

Printed by
Parksons Graphics Pvt. Ltd., Mumbai

movies & tv
streaming
prime
fast & free

amazon

CONTENTS

Introduction **9**

By the Book **15**

Garage Power 20

Rufus at Work 26

Pushing for Profits **31**

Amazon Reviews 39

Beyond Books **43**

Amazon Down 47

Making News 51

Politics and Pandemics **57**

Richest Man in the World 63

Pre-Prime 71

Masks and Hand Sanitizer 75

Selected Bibliography **76**

Glossary **77**

Websites **79**

Index **80**

Introduction

Shortly after the Amazon.com website launched on July 16, 1995, a loud beep echoed through the company's offices near downtown Seattle, Washington. The beep alerted the Amazon.com staff that a customer had made a purchase. The beep sounded six more times that day and was accompanied each time by a cheer from Amazon employees.

OPPOSITE: The iconic observation tower called the Space Needle overlooks downtown Seattle, a city of more than 750,000 people.

But those beeps quickly became more frequent—and more distracting to the small staff. In its first week, the company logged more than $12,000 worth of purchases.

Within a couple weeks, the bell had become so distracting that it had to be disabled. And it would be almost impossible to keep up with sales today. In 2021, the company sold more than 13.5 billion individual items. At least 19 orders are placed on Amazon.com every second. Almost 66,000 products are shipped out from one of the company's

In its early days, Amazon shipped most items in heavy corrugated cardboard boxes.

OPPOSITE The Amazon River carries more fresh water into the oceans than any other river in the world.

more than 200 fulfillment centers around the world every hour.

Like its namesake—the Amazon River in South America—Amazon.com is famous for being the largest. Company founder Jeff Bezos referenced the river on November 1, 1994, the day he registered the URL for his new online bookstore. "This is not only the largest river in the world," he said, "it's many times larger than the next biggest river. It blows all other rivers away."

1993
READINGS IN THE PHILOSOPHICAL PROBLEMS OF PARAPSYCHOLOGY
CALIGARI TRUESPACE2 BIBLE
HEALTH WEALTH George Anders
BIRDS
Managing Finance for Quality
YAN-KIT'S CLASSIC CHINESE COOKBOOK
The Icon Programming Language
The New York Times Crossword Puzzle Dictionary Third Edition
Looking Good in Print
McDermott
LITTLE, BROWN
NORTHERN EXPOSURE BOOK
HIGH-SPEED DIGITAL DESIGN
A HANDBOOK OF BLACK MAGIC
Dictionary of American Quotations
Margaret Miner and Hugh Rawson
At the Crest of the TIDAL WAVE
The COMPLETE KAMA SUTRA
GIETZEN
ADVANCED CYCLE TRADING
Better HANDWRITING
MOSTLY VEGETABLES Susan Costner
QUINN
THE BEST OF THOROUGHBRED HANDICAPPING
MORROW
Benchmarking for Effective Network Management
Palladio THE FOUR BOOKS OF ARCHITECTURE
THE MICROPROCESSOR A Biography MALONE
Eccles/Crane
GOLF DREAMS
GOLF DREAMS
Reinventing Electric Utilities
Angela's Ashes Frank McCourt
THE DILBERT
DAVID FOSTER WALLACE
BORN to REBEL
WORLDLY GOODS
WORLDLY GOODS

By the Book

Drive west. This was the only instruction that Jeff Bezos and his wife, MacKenzie, gave the movers who had packed up their Manhattan apartment in the summer of 1994. Bezos promised to call them with a specific destination the next day. At the age of 30, Bezos had just quit his job as a rising star at a New York investment company. He had a vision for an online bookstore.

OPPOSITE: Jeff Bezos transformed the book-buying experience, turning physical shopping carts into virtual ones.

Bezos knew that he needed to build his headquarters in a city that embraced technology, was flush with recent college graduates, and was near a large book distribution center. So, he called the movers and told them to head for Seattle, Washington. Seattle was the home of software company Microsoft and the University of Washington. It was also just a six-hour drive from Ingram Book Group, one of the largest book distributors in the country.

With MacKenzie driving a 1988 Chevy Blazer they had borrowed from his dad, Bezos rode shotgun and filled spreadsheets with **revenue** projections for his Internet-based business. He was excited about the World Wide Web, which had only begun to be used by the public in the fall of 1993. He could see the potential for online **commerce** and knew that he had to build his business before every other **entrepreneur** also figured that out. He chose books as his business. He knew that they were easy to purchase from publishers and distributors. He knew that books were affordable and that people liked to buy them. And Bezos was confident that building his bookstore on the Web, without the **overhead** of a **brick-and-mortar** store, would allow him to offer better deals than traditional booksellers could.

When they got to Seattle, Bezos and MacKenzie rented a small home with an attached one-car garage. That garage became the company's first office in November 1994. Bezos had recruited two programmers—Sheldon Kaphan and Paul Davis—to work with him. He made desks for all three of them out of plain wooden doors from Home Depot. Then they got busy figuring out the website's technical details, including what it would look like and how it would store information about customers' orders. Bezos, Kaphan, and Davis relied on open-source software to develop the framework for the online bookstore. Open-source software is a set of programs programmers write and then make available to other programmers at no charge.

At the same time, Bezos was trying to secure financial backing for the company. His family had invested almost $250,000 in exchange for **stock** in the business, which was **incorporated** as Amazon.com in February 1995.

Technology drives every part of Amazon's business.

Garage Power

Jeff Bezos had only one requirement when he and his wife were looking for a house to rent in Seattle: It had to have a garage. Many of the entrepreneurs whom Bezos admired had started in their garages—including Steve Jobs, who created Apple with his friend Steve Wozniak in his parents' garage. Perhaps it was a sign of things to come when Amazon's computers and other equipment maxed out the space's electrical capacity in a matter of months. Bezos joked that electricity was the reason companies had to move out of garages. "It's not that they run out of room," he said. "It's that they run out of electrical power."

That was enough money to hire a few employees and to move into a larger space in Seattle's industrial district just in time for the website's official launch on July 16, 1995.

Sales trickled in until Yahoo!, a Web **search engine,** placed Amazon.com on its "What's Cool" list three days after launch. Traffic on the site increased rapidly. At the end of the first week, Amazon.com had tallied $12,438 in orders. At that pace, the company expected revenues of $5 million in its first year. But it needed additional money up front to hire more employees, upgrade equipment, and develop its services.

Bezos was willing to wait for his company to make money—his original business plan had predicted that it would be five years before the company would turn a **profit**. But Amazon.com needed funds to remain in business. With the help of friends, Bezos secured $981,000 in private funding by the end of 1995. And then, thanks to a glowing article about Amazon in the *Wall Street Journal* on May 16, 1996, more investors started calling. Kleiner Perkins Caufield & Byers, a venture capital

TAKEAWAY

Bezos could see the potential for online commerce and knew that he had to build his Web-based business before every other entrepreneur also figured that out.

firm that invested in new tech startups, provided $8 million in exchange for a 13 percent stake in the company.

Bezos was able to hire more managers, warehouse workers, and customer service agents. With the number of employees growing, however, the company had to move into a larger office building in downtown Seattle. It also had to purchase a 93,000-square-foot (8,640-square-meter) warehouse facility. The company's staggering growth led to another move as well: selling shares of Amazon on

Secretary of the Treasury.
HB 84550434 I

the stock market. On May 15, 1997, the day of its **initial public offering**, Amazon raised $54 million. Bezos and his family members—including his mom, dad, brother, and sister—immediately became millionaires. So did many of the employees who had been promised stock as part of their payment package.

By October 1997, just two years after Amazon had launched, the one-millionth customer placed an order. Bezos flew to Japan to personally deliver the two books—a computer

Rufus at Work

When Jeff Bezos hired Eric and Susan Benson to work at Amazon early in its history, he got a third "employee" as well. Every day, the couple brought their pet corgi, Rufus, to the office with them. Rufus became an unofficial mascot for Amazon. Bezos even asked the landlord of one of the company's early buildings to write the dog into the lease. Before any new feature of the website was launched, Rufus had to tap his paw on the keyboard. Although Rufus is now long gone, thousands of other dogs continue to join their owners at Amazon.

text and a biography of Princess Diana—to the customer. At the end of the year, Amazon had made $147.8 million, an 838 percent jump over the previous year. But because it was adding employees, investing in new buildings, and increasing its **marketing** budget, the company again lost more money than it made.

Bezos was under pressure to show a profit. Instead of tightening his belt, however, he made several **acquisitions.** He positioned Amazon as a one-stop shopping site, not just a bookseller. By 1999, Amazon's eight million customers could buy books, music, and DVDs, as well as electronics, toys and games, home improvement products, software, video games, and gifts. The company had 5,000 employees and multiple locations—including sites in Germany and the United Kingdom. But it was still losing money.

That didn't deter the editors of *Time* magazine from naming Bezos the Person of the Year for 1999. Amid rapid growth in online businesses, the magazine described the 35-year-old Internet entrepreneur as "unquestionably, the king of cybercommerce." It lauded his efforts to help "build the foundation of our future."

With a credit card and a few clicks on a computer, consumers can buy almost anything on Amazon.

Pushing for Profits

The unchecked optimism surrounding Web-based businesses between 1995 and 2000 led to widespread adoption of the Internet as part of daily life, for both business and pleasure. Shoppers were becoming more comfortable spending money online, and investors were eager to put large amounts of money into new start-up companies built on websites.

OPPOSITE: In 2005, under the leadership of Jeff Bezos, Amazon celebrated its 10th year on a high note.

Those investments and high expectations for profitability caused the stock market to skyrocket. But in the spring of 2000, just as Bezos was planning for Amazon.com to show its first profit, the financial bubble building around the surge in dot-com companies burst. Many of the start-ups that had received hopeful funding from investors hadn't able to turn a profit. Around the same time, interest rates started going up, which made it harder to borrow money. In reaction, the stock market index plunged by more than 700 percent in a matter of weeks. Dozens of new dot-com companies disappeared almost immediately. Others struggled to stay afloat.

Amazon.com was in a better position than most, but it didn't escape the bust unharmed. The value of its stock took a steep drop, and shareholders were angry. The media, which had praised Bezos for his clever ideas just a few months earlier, turned critical. The company was labeled with such nicknames as "Amazon.bomb" and "Amazon.toast" as critics predicted the company's collapse. "You go from Internet poster child to Internet whipping boy," Bezos said in a *Fortune* magazine article in December 2000. "It takes, like, 30 seconds."

The pressure to show a profit ramped up. As 2000 ended, Bezos sent an email to all Amazon employees announcing the company's internal goal to turn a profit within the next year. "We're aiming to have sales of $5 billion, produce

Fulfillment center employees receive goods, pick and pack orders, and ship those orders to customers.

amazon.com
amazon.com
12X916
16X12X4

over $1 billion in gross profits, and achieve solid operating profitability," he wrote.

Of course, to make that happen, Bezos had to make deep cuts to Amazon's operations. He laid off 1,300 workers, closed 2 warehouses and a customer-service center, and brought in experts to help streamline the business's processes. He also purged products that weren't profitable from the site's offerings. Then, he forged a partnership with bookstore giant Borders to foster cooperation, rather than competition, between the two businesses.

But the company continued to struggle. Bezos's goal went unrealized. Amazon reported a staggering net loss of $567 million in 2001 and of $149 million in 2002. In each year, a strong holiday season had led to fourth-quarter profits, which were encouraging. And although it was still limping along financially,

Amazon was now being called a survivor. Many online retailers, including Boo.com and Pets.com, had shut down completely. Amazon was one of the few e-commerce companies still in business after the devastating dot-com bust.

Amazon's progress toward profitability continued in 2003. Customers responded positively to newly implemented price cuts and the addition of clothing and accessories to Amazon's inventory. They were also drawn to the offer of free shipping on certain orders over $25. But it was a book that helped propel the company to its first profitable year: *Harry Potter and the Order of the Phoenix*, the fifth book in the popular Harry Potter series by author J. K. Rowling. Customers were able to place advance orders for the book starting on January 15. By the time it was officially released on June 21, more than 1.3 million copies had been pre-ordered worldwide—more than any other product that had been available during Amazon's eight-year history.

Those sales, combined with a fantastic holiday season and growth in international sales—Amazon had sites in six countries, including Canada, Japan, and France—the company reported a profit of $35 million in 2003. Having met that critical **benchmark**, Amazon suddenly seemed to be able to make money easily. On a single day during the 2004 holiday season, customers ordered more than 2.8 million items from the website. That

Amazon Reviews

One of the earliest features added to Amazon.com was the ability to add reviews, which Shel Kaphan coded over a weekend in June 1995. Although Kaphan and other Amazon employees wrote the first book reviews, it didn't take long for others to join in—or to add a bit of humor. Shoppers have left creative reviews for everything from Bic pens to gummi bears. One long, descriptive review of sugar-free gummi bears ended with this line:

"Not only did they cause me to fail my final test, but the anguish I experienced is something I wouldn't wish upon anyone, not even my worst enemy."

day helped push total sales for the year up to $6.9 billion.

Bezos was in a celebratory mood for Amazon's 10th birthday in 2005. In addition to hosting a party that featured famed musicians Bob Dylan and Norah Jones, the company introduced Amazon Prime. This new program provided free two-day and discounted shipping for an annual fee of $79. Although Prime became quite popular with customers, its rollout was worrisome to many inside the company and to Wall Street analysts. They saw it eating away at overall revenues. During the first three months of 2005, for example, Amazon spent $167 million on shipping costs. Only a fraction of that was paid back by customers. Add to that the cost of hiring computer programmers to perfect Amazon's search engine and further tweak the site's features. There was also a growing market-

TAKEAWAY

> "If we take care of customers, the stock will take care of itself in the long term."

ing budget, which was dedicated almost entirely to email campaigns and promotions. Bezos considered all of those initiatives part of his plan to put customers first, instead of focusing on profits. "If we take care of customers, the stock will take care of itself in the long term," he said.

To prove his point, Bezos spent most of 2006 expanding the services, products, and features available through Amazon.com. In November, the company was voted number one in customer service in a National Retail Survey. December sales eclipsed all previous holiday sales records, thanks in large part to products such as Apple iPods and Nintendo Wii gaming systems. Even so, the company's profits of $190 million were considered a disappointment.

Prime
337

Beyond Books

Despite disappointing revenues, Bezos had a reason to be optimistic about his company's future in 2007. For three years, Amazon's developers had been secretly working on what they called "Project A": a portable electronic reader that would be able to **download** digital content such as books, articles, and more.

OPPOSITE: Started in 2017, Amazon Air (originally Amazon Prime Air) transports goods between the company's distribution centers.

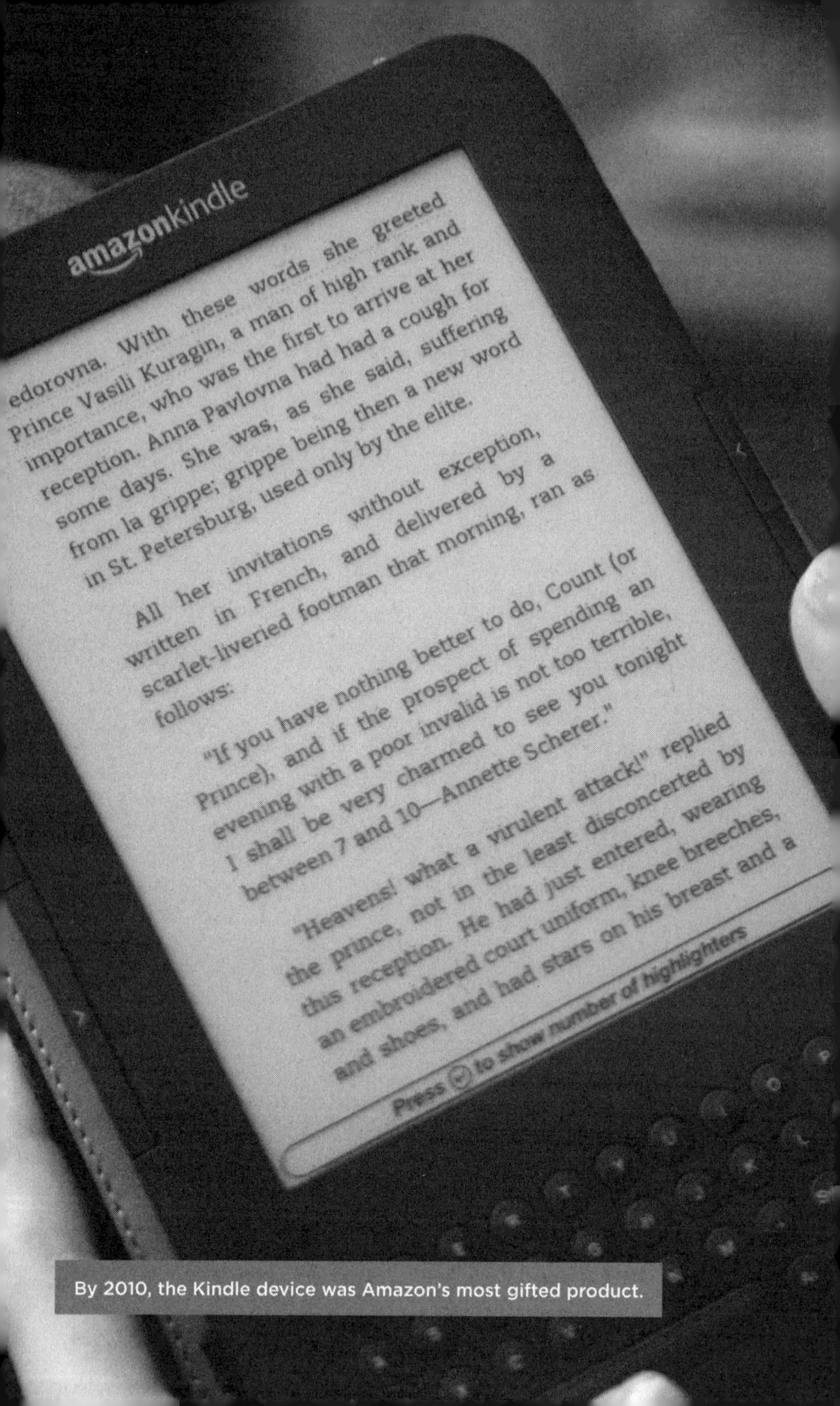

By 2010, the Kindle device was Amazon's most gifted product.

TAKEAWAY

"The baby boomers have a love affair with paper. But the next-gen people, in their 20s and below, do everything on a screen."

Similar products made by companies such as Sony were already in the market, but Amazon believed its product would provide a better experience for readers. On November 19, 2007, Amazon released the Kindle—its first self-made product. It immediately started selling more than 90,000 digital books, including almost all the current *New York Times* bestsellers and new releases, at a flat rate of $9.99.

One of the Kindle's main distinctions from earlier e-readers was its ability to download books without connecting to a computer. That high-tech convenience, combined with its compact size and easy-to-read lighted screen, was especially appealing to a younger audience. "The baby boomers have a love affair with paper," said novelist James Patterson when the Kindle was launched. "But the next-gen people, in their 20s and below, do everything on a screen."

All 250,000 of the $399 Kindles in Amazon's original inventory sold out within hours of the launch. The replacement batch disappeared just as quickly when popular talk show host Oprah Winfrey had Bezos on her show. Digital books accounted for 10 percent of Amazon's total book sales for the year, even though only 200,000 titles, just a fraction of the millions of books available on Amazon, were ready for download. Readers had clearly embraced the Kindle technology. "This is the most important thing we've ever done," Bezos

Amazon Down

It can be frustrating when a website has technical difficulties. For an e-commerce site such as Amazon.com, it can also be quite costly. Consider what happened in August 2013, when the site stopped working for almost 40 minutes. Shoppers saw this message: "Oops! We're very sorry, but we're having trouble doing what you just asked us to do. Please give us another chance—click the Back button on your browser and try your request again." By the time service was restored, the company had lost almost $5 million in sales, considering that in the previous quarter they had recorded $15.7 billion in sales, which equals about $120,000 every minute.

said. "It's so ambitious to take something as highly evolved as the book and improve on it—and maybe even change the way people read."

Amazon released an upgraded version of the Kindle in 2009 to keep up with new e-readers released by Barnes & Noble and Sony. By that time, almost 400,000 digital books were available on the website. Amazon had purchased audiobook company Audible in 2008, gaining access to its immense library of digital materials. For the first

Amazon's smartphone, called Fire Phone, was not a hit with consumers.

time in company history, e-books sold better than printed books during the holiday shopping season.

Even as developers continued working on upgrades to the Kindle, "Project B" was already in the works: a smartphone. Work on the project began in 2010, just as Apple was releasing the

TAKEAWAY

> "It's so ambitious to take something as highly evolved as the book and improve on it—and maybe even change the way people read."

iPhone 4. Despite efforts to keep it under wraps, media speculation was rampant in the years leading up to the Fire Phone's release in July 2014. One of the stories reported that the phone would be offered for free to Amazon Prime members. In fact, the phones cost $199 for the 32GB version and $299 for the 64GB version. Some of the earliest buyers were rewarded for their purchase with a free Prime membership.

Unlike the Kindle, however, Amazon's Fire Phone didn't lure customers away from the existing smartphone options. Its most unique attribute was "Dynamic Perspective," which used four front-facing cameras and a gyroscope to track the user's eyes and give the screen an almost 3D sense of depth. Even that feature didn't create enough buzz around the phone. By August 2015, the Fire Phone was no longer available on Amazon.com.

By then, however, Amazon's attention had shifted to "Project D," its third successful hardware launch (Project C was abandoned before coming to market). In November 2014, the company released the Amazon Echo, a smart speaker that was powered by Alexa, the **artificial intelligence** "voice" of the product. Although it was first available only to Amazon Prime members, by the 2015 holiday season, the Echo device was available in more than 3,000 retail stores throughout the United States. That year, more than one million Echoes were sold

Making News

In August 2013, Jeff Bezos offered to pay $250 million of his own money to purchase *The Washington Post*, a newspaper published in Washington, D.C., that was struggling financially. Bezos decided to make the newspaper a private company instead of a publicly traded one. As such, he didn't have to report earnings to shareholders. Although Bezos was too busy running Amazon to get involved in the day-to-day operations of *The Washington Post*, some assumed that he was using it to push his own agenda. President Donald Trump accused Bezos of using the newspaper to push for his own personal interests and to help Amazon.

during the holidays. A year later, more than nine million were sold worldwide during the holiday season alone, making 2016 the company's best holiday shopping season to date.

As sales of the Echo and the Dot, its smaller companion smart speaker, were surging, so was Amazon's workforce. Since its humble beginnings in Bezos's garage, the company had steadily outgrown each office space it occupied. In 2010, Amazon moved its corporate headquarters to a towering 1.6 million-square-foot (148,645-sq-m) building in an industrial neighborhood north of

Seattle's downtown district. That building, which occupied a full city block and featured a set of three glass spheres (akin to the pyramids fronting the entrance to the Louvre Museum in Paris, France), provided space for more than 10,000 employees. But even that wasn't enough room for Amazon's continued growth.

So, in 2017, Amazon started searching for a location for its second headquarters—known throughout the company simply as "HQ2." By the deadline for proposals, 238 cities across the United States and Canada had submitted bids full of incentives to entice Amazon to choose them, including tax cuts and prime real estate options. Becoming the site of an Amazon headquarters would bring up to 50,000 jobs and billions of dollars to whichever city was selected. Major metropolitan areas pulled out all the stops to woo the company. New York City lit up landmarks such as the Empire State Building and One World Trade Center in "Amazon Orange"; New York's governor offered to change his name to Andrew "Amazon" Cuomo if the company choose to settle in the Big Apple. "The case for New York City is simple: We are the global capital of commerce, culture, and innovation," New York mayor Bill de Blasio wrote in a letter to Bezos.

A year after starting its search, Amazon announced that it would split its second headquarters between two cities: Long Island City, New York, and Arlington, Virginia. Each city would be home to 25,000 employees and receive an investment of more than $2.5 billion from Amazon.

The Spheres outside Amazon corporate headquarters in Seattle

Politics and Pandemics

Amazon started its 25th year in 2019 at the top of its game. It accounted for almost half of all online sales in the United States and employed more than 640,000 people worldwide. But that success came with growing pains, as was evidenced by the negative reaction to its HQ2 plans in New York City. Although many leaders had gone to great lengths to lure the company to the city, not everyone was thrilled about Amazon's arrival in the Big Apple.

OPPOSITE: Face masks were a highly sought-after item on Amazon during the COVID-19 pandemic of 2020.

Amazon's intense warehouse tracking methods and fast pace can lead to employee injuries and burnout.

On the day after Long Island City was announced as one of two locations for a new Amazon campus, residents started protesting. They were joined by local politicians who disagreed with the tax cuts and other benefits that had been offered to the company. **Union** officials and other advocates were critical of the way Amazon treated employees.

In the weeks that followed, opposition grew. Amazon tried holding rallies with supporters and sending fliers to residents. Nothing helped. On February 14, 2019, Amazon withdrew its HQ2 offer from New York, citing a lack of support from local and state politicians. It would focus its new headquarters solely in Arlington, Virginia, as well as a smaller hub in Nashville, Tennessee.

But within a year, discussions of Amazon's physical locations would become far less prominent. When the COVID-19 pandemic started in early 2020, Amazon's online shopping model saved the day for customers who no longer had access to necessities in their local stores. It was the perfect alternative for those who weren't comfortable going to public places, where they could possibly contract the virus. More people started working from home, and schools established remote learning programs.

During the pandemic, brick-and-mortar stores saw a big drop in customer traffic.

Online shopping for everything from groceries and cleaning supplies to soundproof headphones and office supplies took off. So did Amazon's profits. Thanks to a 37 percent growth of sales in the third quarter of 2020, the company recorded quarterly profits of $6.3 billion—an increase of 197 percent over the third quarter the previous year.

It wasn't just retail sales that were thriving. The efforts Amazon had made to vary its offerings over the years paid off during the pandemic. Amazon Web Services, which had started in 2003 as a platform to host e-commerce sites for other businesses, grew tremendously as more businesses looked to move sales online. Prime Video, the company's streaming service, saw a dramatic increase in the number of subscriptions. More families stayed

Richest Man in the World

In July 2018, Jeff Bezos's **net worth** grew to more than $150 billion, which earned him the title of "richest man in the world." He stayed on top for the next two years, eclipsing the $200 billion mark in 2020, thanks to Amazon's sales during the pandemic. By 2023, Bezos had handed the crown to Tesla founder Elon Musk and slipped to third place among richest people. But by then, Bezos had decided to donate most of his money to causes he cares about—primarily fighting climate change and bridging social and political divisions.

In 2020, Amazon employee numbers jumped more than 60 percent worldwide over 2019.

home to binge-watch shows and movies during pandemic-related lockdowns and quarantines.

To keep up with demand, Amazon announced that it would be hiring up to 100,000 more employees, many of them warehouse workers. Those opportunities were a boon to retail workers and others who had been laid off. But they also put thousands of people near each other in crowded warehouse settings. Concerns about safety conditions led to a walkout by employees at a Staten Island warehouse in March 2020. Employees at locations in Michigan and Illinois soon did the same. Workers across the company took to social media to voice their complaints, which led to discussions about organizing to protect themselves. "We need to unionize nationwide to have a voice for health and better working conditions," an employee from Texas posted on a Facebook group for Amazon workers.

Amazon fiercely opposed the unionization efforts. Unions give employees negotiating power that can force a company to increase salaries and benefits and upgrade safety protocols, which can have a negative impact on profitability. Amazon invested millions of dollars campaigning against union votes at several locations across the country. By the end of 2022, only one location,

Calls to unionize at Amazon have been part of the company's history since the beginning.

Jeff Bezos (*second from left*) and crew of Blue Origin's first manned flight, 2021

a warehouse in Staten Island, had successfully voted to unionize.

Amidst the pandemic and employee unrest, Jeff Bezos stepped down as Amazon CEO on July 5, 2021—exactly 27 years after launching the company. Although he would stay on as executive chairman, he was letting go of day-to-day operations. He wanted to focus on **philanthropic** projects, climate change, and space exploration—including a trip to outer space in a rocket built by his company, Blue

411
AT&T
DO NOT
BLOCK
DRIVEWAY
352234
20

Pre-Prime

Before there was Amazon Prime, there was Super Saver Shipping. It allowed Amazon shoppers to pay a lower rate for shipping because their orders waited until there was room on the trucks, which sometimes delayed delivery. The reduced delivery cost led some shoppers to add more products to their online carts. Amazon believed that Prime's subscription-based free delivery would lead to even more sales. They were right. Prime created "Amazon Addicts" who shopped for books, clothing, and food on the site. "It was really about changing people's mentality so they wouldn't shop anywhere else," said Vijay Ravindran, the director of ordering services when Prime was introduced in 2005.

Origin. "I've never had more energy, and this isn't about retiring," Bezos wrote in a letter to employees announcing the change early in 2021. "I'm super passionate about the impact I think these organizations can have."

Bezos named Andy Jassy, who had worked for Amazon since 1997, as his **successor**. Jassy inherited a company that was experiencing record sales and huge profits. But it was also a company that had been embattled by lawsuits and unionization efforts and was still figuring out how to manage operations during a pandemic.

TAKEAWAY

> "I've never had more energy, and this isn't about retiring. I'm super passionate about the impact I think these organizations can have."

Although most of those factors were out of his control, Jassy's first year was marked by a 40 percent plunge in Amazon's stock price—the biggest decline since the dot-com bust in 2001.

Things got worse in 2022. Record **inflation**, rising interest rates, and major supply chain issues wreaked havoc on Amazon's earnings and led to one of the company's worst financial performances in its history. Jassy was forced to take a large pay cut himself, but he also had to eliminate thousands of jobs. By spring of 2023, more than 27,000 job cuts had been announced.

Construction of the company's HQ2 facility in Arlington, Virginia, had been paused.

Amazon has been through similar ups and downs in its history and has proven that it can come through better than before. As it invests more in new ideas, from robots and drones to space-age satellite networks, it will continue to search for the next big thing that will propel it into the future—and allow it to continue providing everything customers need, delivered right to their doors.

Masks and Hand Sanitizer

When the COVID-19 pandemic hit in the spring of 2020, Amazon shoppers started stocking up on supplies such as toilet paper, cleaning wipes, and face masks. They were often shocked by the prices. Third-party merchants, who sell items through Amazon, were listing 8-ounce (227-gram) bottles of hand sanitizer, which usually sold for less than $3.00, for almost $30.00. One man had stockpiled more than 17,000 bottles of hand sanitizer, intending to sell them on Amazon for a profit. Several sellers were fined for price gouging—the practice of increasing prices of in-demand goods to an unreasonable level—and Amazon suspended more than 10,000 accounts for inflating prices.

Selected Bibliography

"Amazon.com, Inc. history, profile, and history video." CompaniesHistory.com. Accessed May 20, 2023. https://www.companieshistory.com/amazon-com.

Bryar, Colin, and Bill Carr. *Working Backwards: Insights, Stories and Secrets from Inside Amazon*. New York: St. Martin's Press, 2021.

Dumaine, Brian. *Bezonomics: How Amazon Is Changing Our Lives and What the World's Best Companies Are Learning from It*. New York: Scribner, 2020.

Ramo, Joshua Cooper. "1999 Person of the Year: Jeffrey P. Bezos." *Time* magazine., December 27, 1999.

Stone, Brad. *Amazon Unbound: Jeff Bezos and the Invention of a Global Empire*. New York: Simon & Schuster, 2022.

---. *The Everything Store: Jeff Bezos and the Age of Amazon*. New York: Back Bay Books, 2013.

Glossary

acquisition the purchase of a company by another company

artificial intelligence the ability of computer systems to perform tasks that normally require human intelligence, such as speech recognition and decision-making

benchmark a point against which similar things can be compared

brick-and-mortar describing businesses that operate out of an actual building, as opposed to those that operate online

commerce the activity of buying and selling

download to transfer data to a computer system from a separate remote system, such as a website or email service

entrepreneur a person who organizes a new business venture and assumes the risks associated with it

incorporate to legally form into a company

inflation the increase in prices and decline in the purchasing value of money

initial public offering the process of offering shares in a company to the public for the first time

marketing	the process of promoting products or services
net worth	the total wealth of an individual or company
overhead	the expenses associated with maintaining a building, including utility costs, property taxes, and insurance
philanthropic	promoting the welfare of others, usually through the donation of money to causes that help people in need
profit	the amount of money that a business keeps after subtracting expenses from revenues
revenue	the money earned by a company; another word for income
search engine	a computer program that finds and retrieves files or data from a computer network or the Internet based on search terms entered by a user
stock	shared ownership in a company by many people who buy shares, or portions, of stock, hoping the company will make a profit and the stock value will increase
successor	the person who comes after another leader
union	an organized group of workers who ensure members have fair wages, benefits, and working conditions

Websites

About Amazon
https://www.aboutamazon.com
Read news related to the company, including new products and corporate updates.

Business
https://www.timeforkids.com/g56/sections/business
Learn more about successful businesses and the people who run them.

Jeff Bezos
https://www.biography.com/business-leaders/jeff-bezos
Discover how Jeff Bezos went from a kid in New Mexico to one of the richest men in the world.

Index

Alexa, 50
"Amazon Addicts," 71
Amazon Air, 43
Amazon Prime, 40, 43, 49, 50, 71
Amazon River, 13
Amazon Web Services, 62
Arlington, Virginia, 54, 60, 74
Audible, 47
Benson, Eric and Susan, 26
Bezos, Jeff, 13, 15, 16, 17, 18, 20, 22, 23, 25, 26, 27, 28, 31, 32, 33, 36, 40, 41, 43, 46, 47, 51, 52, 54, 63, 68, 69, 72
Bezos, MacKenzie, 15, 16, 17
books
  audio, 47
  digital, 43, 45, 46, 47
  Harry Potter and the Order of the Phoenix, 38
COVID-19, 57, 60–62, 73, 75
customer numbers, 9, 25, 27, 28
customer service, 23, 36, 41
Davis, Paul, 17, 18
delivery. *See* shipping
Dot, 52
dot-com bust, 32–33, 37, 73
downtime costs, 47
Echo, 50, 52
employees, 9, 21, 22, 23, 25, 26, 27, 28, 33, 34, 39, 53, 54, 58, 59, 64, 65, 66, 69, 72
e-readers. *See* Kindle
Fire Phone, 48–50
Fortune magazine, 33
fulfillment centers, 13, 33, 34–35
headquarters, corporate, 16, 52–53
headquarters, second (HQ2), 53, 54, 60
holiday seasons, 36, 38, 41, 48, 50, 52
investors, 18, 22–23, 31, 32
Jassy, Andy, 72, 73
Kaphan, Sheldon, 17, 18, 39
Kindle, 43, 44, 45–47, 48, 49
launch date (site), 9, 21
name origin, 13
Nashville, Tennessee, 60
New York City, 15, 54, 57, 59
New York State, 54, 59
offices, 9, 17, 20, 26, 52

pandemic. *See* COVID-19
price gouging, 75
Prime Video, 62
profits, company, 22, 27, 32, 33, 36, 37, 38, 41, 61, 62, 66, 72, 75
"Project A." *See* Kindle
"Project B." *See* Fire Phone
"Project C," 50
"Project D." *See* Echo
reviews, 39
Rufus, 26
Seattle, Washington, 9, 16, 17, 20, 21, 23, 53, 55
services, 22, 41, 62
shipping, 10, 11, 13, 34, 37, 40, 70, 71, 74
smartphones, 48, 49
smart speakers, 50, 52
stock, 18, 23, 25, 32, 41, 73
Super Saver Shipping, 71
Time magazine, 28
unions, 59, 66, 67, 69, 72
warehouses, 23, 36, 58, 65, 66, 69
The Washington Post, 51
Yahoo!, 21

More Titles from the Creative Companies Series

Jaico's creative companies series explores how today's great companies operate and inspires young readers to become the entrepreneurs and businessmen of tomorrow.

Amazon

Jeff Bezos founded Amazon in 1994 in a garage in Seattle, Washington, as an online bookstore. On July 16, 1995, Bezos launched the site, named after the vast Amazon River, and invited 300 friends to beta test it. Within 30 days, Amazon sold books across the U.S. and 45 countries, achieving meteoric success without press promotion. Today, Amazon is an e-commerce giant, offering a vast array of products and services while continuously innovating under Bezos's visionary leadership.

Apple

Did you know, Apple—the company behind your iPod, iPad, iPhone—began as a project shared by two ambitious boys in their computer club? When Steve Wozniak designed a computer in 1976, his friend Steve Jobs immediately saw its potential for a mass market. They found their first 'customer' at their local hobby club meeting and Apple Computer was born. Over the next 30-plus years, their company would transform the computer industry.

Google

This is the inspiring story of Larry Page and Sergey Brin, the founders of Google, who first met at Stanford University, in 1995. Most people would not even be aware of the fact that the very first Google office was in a friend's rented garage. Page and Brin soon began working on a likely doctoral thesis, which involved an attempt to download the complete World Wide Web, after which they would create a way to search the web, with the help of links. After many issues that involved budgeting and design, Google came into being.

Microsoft

Bill Gates was in his second year of college at Harvard when he and his partner Paul Allen launched their own computer software company. Throughout their years at Lakeside School, Bill Gates and Paul Allen spent as much time as they could working on computers, becoming good friends in the process. Their company's impact has been such that the name 'Microsoft' has become virtually synonymous with computer software.

Netflix

Netflix was founded in 1997 by Reed Hastings and Marc Randolph in California as a DVD rental-by-mail service. Hastings was inspired after incurring a $40 late fee on a VHS rental, sparking the idea for a subscription-based model. In 2007, Netflix pivoted to online streaming, offering on-demand entertainment. By 2013, it expanded into original programming with hits like House of Cards. Today, Netflix is a global streaming powerhouse, revolutionizing how audiences consume movies and TV shows across the world.

Spotify

Spotify was founded in 2006 by Daniel Ek and Martin Lorentzon in Stockholm, Sweden, as a response to music piracy. They envisioned a legal platform offering instant, affordable access to a vast music library. Launched in 2008, Spotify introduced a freemium model with ads and premium subscriptions. Its curated playlists and personalized recommendations reshaped music consumption. Today, Spotify is a global leader in audio streaming, boasting millions of tracks and podcasts, transforming how listeners discover and enjoy music worldwide..

Tesla

Tesla was founded in 2003 by Martin Eberhard and Marc Tarpenning, with Elon Musk joining shortly after as an investor and chairman. Named after inventor Nikola Tesla, the company aimed to revolutionize transportation with electric vehicles. In 2008, Tesla launched the Roadster, proving EVs could be high-performance. Musk's leadership expanded Tesla's vision to sustainable energy solutions, including solar products and battery storage. Today, Tesla leads the EV industry, pushing innovation and advancements in autonomous driving.

Starbucks

Starbucks was founded in 1971 by Jerry Baldwin, Zev Siegl, and Gordon Bowker in Seattle, Washington, as a single store selling high-quality coffee beans and equipment. Inspired by Italian coffee culture, Howard Schultz joined in 1982 and later transformed Starbucks into a café-centric brand, emphasizing premium coffee experiences. The first café opened in 1984, revolutionizing coffee consumption. Today, Starbucks operates thousands of locations globally.

JAICO PUBLISHING HOUSE

Elevate Your Life. Transform Your World.

ESTABLISHED IN 1946, Jaico Publishing House is home to world-transforming authors such as Robin Sharma, Sadhguru, Osho, the Dalai Lama, Deepak Chopra, Eknath Easwaran, Paramhansa Yogananda, Devdutt Pattanaik, Radhakrishnan Pillai, Morgan Housel, Napoleon Hill, John Maxwell, Brian Tracy, and Stephen Hawking.

Our late founder Mr. Jaman Shah first established Jaico as a book distribution company. Sensing that independence was around the corner, he aptly named his company Jaico ('Jai' means victory in Hindi). In order to service the significant demand for affordable books in a developing nation, Mr. Shah initiated Jaico's own publications. Jaico was India's first publisher of paperback books in the English language.

While self-help; religion and philosophy; mind, body and spirit; and business titles form the cornerstone of our non-fiction list, we publish an exciting range of current affairs, history, biography, art and architecture, travel, and popular science books as well. Our renewed focus on popular fiction is evident in our new titles by a host of fresh young talent from India and abroad.

Jaico's translations division publishes select bestselling titles in over 10 regional languages including Gujarati, Hindi, Kannada, Malayalam, Marathi, Tamil, and Telugu. These include titles from renowned national and international authors like Sudha Murthy, Gaur Gopal Das, Swami Mukundananda, Jay Shetty, Simon Sinek, Ankur Warikoo and Jeff Keller.

Visit our Website

Boasting one of India's largest book distribution networks, Jaico has its headquarters in Mumbai, with branches in Ahmedabad, Bangalore, Chennai, Delhi, Hyderabad, and Kolkata. This network ensures that our books reach all parts of the country, both urban and rural.